The Summer THAT CHANGED MY LIFE

a true, inspiring testament
of a young college student,
who one summer day took a journey
that carried her to the ends of the
earth, to the presence of God.

SHANILE SHARAY GOGGINS
with Benita Taylor

THE SUMMER THAT CHANGED MY LIFE
a true inspiring testament of a young college student, who one summer day would take a journey that would carry her to the ends of the earth, to the presence of God.

v3.0

Outskirts Press, Inc.
http://www.outskirtspress.com

ISBN: 978-1-4327-4209-6

PRINTED IN THE UNITED STATES OF AMERICA

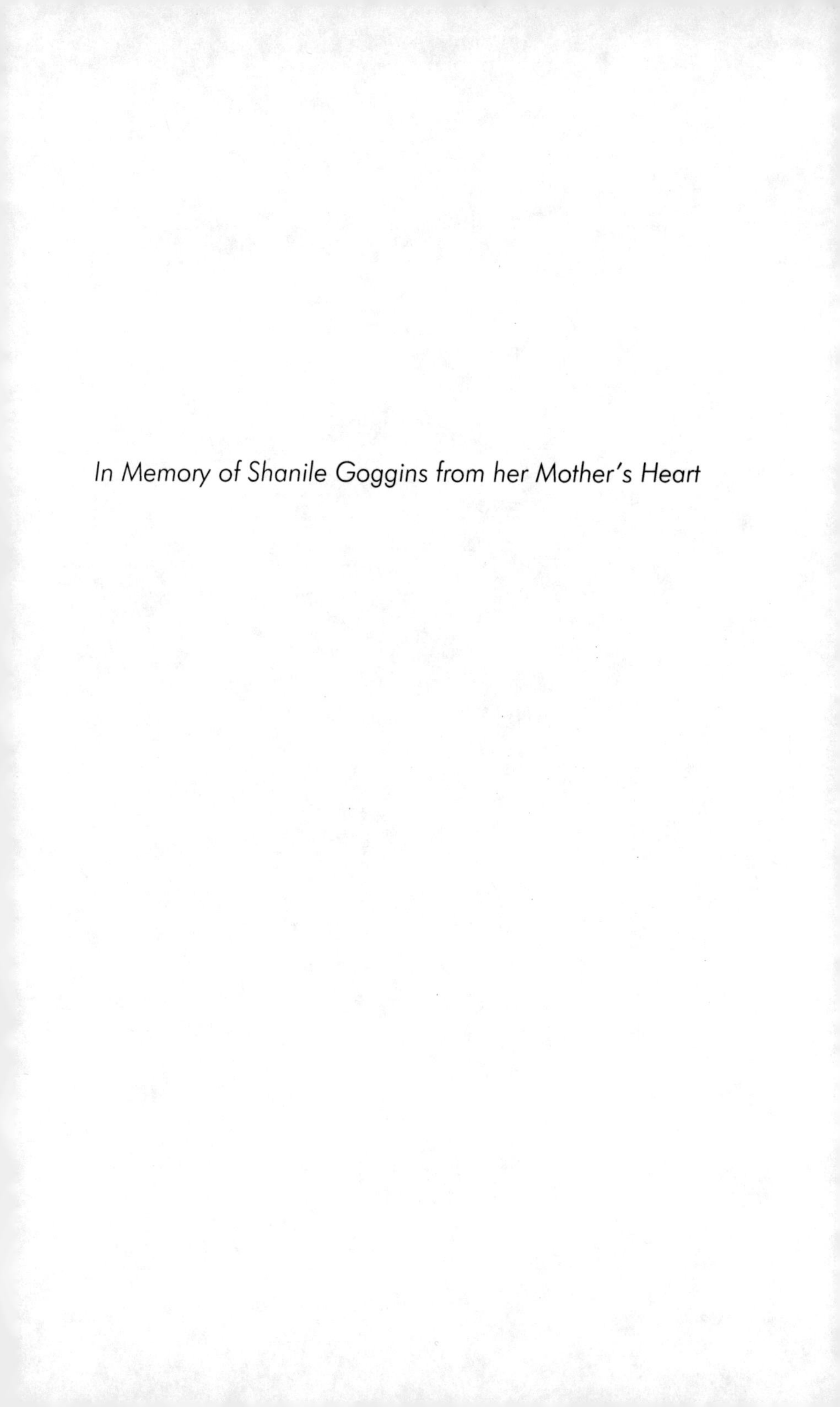

In Memory of Shanile Goggins from her Mother's Heart

Contents

Introduction

My name is Benita Taylor. I am the mother of Shanile Goggins and the author of this book. It was Shanile who decided to share this story with the world, a story about a horrific disease that brings tremendous suffering. Shanile documented on a daily basis the battle she was going through, and how it changed her, mentally and physically.

At the age of nineteen, Shanile was diagnosed with cancer. She continued to pursue a college education and a difficult job at the post office until the battle weakened her. She used to dread going to the hospital because the nurses would get frustrated when they could not find or penetrate her delicate veins. Their frustration, which was often expressed in rude remarks, inflicted discomfort.

Shanile underwent two stem-cell transplants, the second of which she did not survive. She was a very strong-willed person who loved the Lord. She spoke without restraint, but with compassion and thoughtfulness. She passed on to the next life in my arms and in the presence of her brother Michael, and her stepfather, Kevin, at 11:55 a.m.

As her mother, I feel compelled to pursue Shanile's goal of sharing her story with the world. I knew she was special when she was born. She could see angels. One of the angels was in the form of a glowing lion that appeared to her at the age of seven. On that special day she happened to be playing with toys on the floor when all of a sudden, huge paws, covered in fur, stomped right in front of her. The lion told her to not be afraid because he would not hurt her. He said that he was her guardian and would always be around when she needed help because she was special. She said that he turned and walked right through the door.

When she grew older, Shanile had another experience with an angel. She happened to be lying in bed when she saw an angel with big wings and a long gown. The angel of the Lord came to tell her how the devil was kicked out of heaven. She said that the wall in her bedroom turned into a chalkboard. This particular angel carried a long rod in his hand. He told her heaven was where the devil used to live. The devil's name was Lucifer. The angel told her

God is holy and powerful, and nothing bad could come near the Almighty. The angel said the devil wanted to take over God and his kingdom. The holy angel of God said God perceived the devil's thoughts and banished him from heaven. Then the angel began drawing beautiful stars as he described the devil falling and falling, eventually into a star. The angel described how the devil thought he was going to stay in the sky, but the star erupted, and he fell to the earth. The angel turned and looked at Shanile. He told her to stay strong and avoid all evil. Sharing her experiences with her family about angels made Shanile very happy.

I feel that God was definitely preparing my daughter for a truly divine battle with Hodgkin's lymphoma. She attended Christian schools so that she could learn more about our lord, Jesus Christ. As she went through chemo, she worked at a part-time job and attended college.

One day, when she was working in a department store, her aunt stopped by to check on her. Two happy, elderly people walked up to Shanile and embraced her. They asked how she was feeling. They looked at Shanile's aunt and told her Shanile was a good girl, and they loved her. They left the store without making any purchases. It was as if they knew her.

Two years went by and Shanile's aunt had a dream the week Shanile died. In the dream the two elderly people walked up to her smiling and whispering to each other.

Shanile's aunt told the couple they looked familiar, and they said, "Yes, we visited the store and spoke to you about Shanile." Shanile's aunt nodded quickly in agreement. The couple then said they were in the store that particular day to take half of Shanile's pain away. "Now we are back to take the rest of it," they said. At that point Shanile's aunt asked, "Who are you?" The couple said they were angels. Later in the dream, Shanile's aunt said she saw Shanile in bed and her spirit floated out of her body and hovered in the air over her body in the presence of holy angels. She said the angels were glowing and sitting next to the bed. Shanile's spirit floated toward them and gave them a big hug.

When Shanile's aunt told me about her dream and experience, I knew in my heart Shanile was leaving, and her time on earth was over. Her work had been accomplished. Now it was time for her to join Jesus in a beautiful land, free of pain and covered with radiant, green grass, and a glass house that was full of holy harmony. Shanile saw the house in her dreams. I feel blessed by God that she was able to share her dreams with me. To see a child suffer—as a parent there is nothing you can do. You can support the child and you can love her. You have the power to wash her body to keep her clean, put lotion on her and feed her, but keeping your child alive comes from God. I prayed, fasted, cried, and meditated for God to spare the life of my child.

Do not be afraid of death. Jesus conquered death. Shanile would like me to tell people who are struggling to keep their faith in God at all times, and he will deliver them from all of their trials and sufferings in this world.

Shanile died on Friday. She visited my niece Tonya in a vision. Tonya could not see her but heard her voice. Shanile said, "Tonya I know you are not going to believe this, but I am really here. You must take your children and get them baptized in the name of Jesus, the Father, Son, and Holy Spirit." At that point Shanile said, "Did you see all the mess they put on my face? I cannot stay long. I must go visit my friends and my mom." Tonya said the voice then stopped speaking.

God took my daughter out of all her pain. He set her free to live again in his glorious kingdom. I have to remember that God's ways are not my ways. God sent his only son, Jesus, from heaven to give his life for Shanile, me, you, and the world so we can join him at his holy table. He had to undo the sin that Adam and Eve had committed. Jesus conquered death. So, when our loved ones pass, we cannot say God did not grant life because he did.

CHAPTER 1

The Summer That Changed My Life

I was a typical Ohio State student on the Newark campus when very unexpectedly, I was diagnosed with stage-four—terminal—Hodgkin's disease. At that time in my life I was devoting all of my attention to raising my GPA score, and graduating with a bachelor's degree. I was preparing myself to do battle in the real world with a good job placement but was not prepared to battle for my life.

In my second year of college I worked part-time at the Child Development Center across the street from my campus apartment. Spring quarter had just ended, and I planned to attend college part time during the summer quarter while working full time at the center. Unfortunately my summer plans came to an abrupt end, and my life was dramatically changed on June 17, 2004. I arrived at work at 9:00 a.m.

and was placed in a classroom with only three children. Within the first couple of hours there I felt a very violent pain in my chest. The pain was beyond my imagination. It was so intense that I thought I was enduring spontaneous combustion. It felt as if someone had turned on a flaming furnace inside my chest. Breathing frantically, I lunged to the mirror to see if my image somehow depicted the torment I was experiencing. I knew something was definitely wrong. As I examined myself, looking closely in the mirror, I could see no signs that I needed emergency care. I attempted to calm myself by lying face down on the carpet and controlling my breathing for about an hour. I did not call for help because the children were under control, playing tic-tack-toe and writing on the chalk board. I continued working until 3:30 p.m. My scheduled shift was from nine to five. Summer enrolment was slow because of vacations.

On the forty-five-minute route home during rush hour I could not help thinking of a dream I had had about drinking lots of water. In my dream, a masculine voice came from a tree in a forest and told me to drink lots of water. As I remembered the dream, a storm of sadness enveloped me like the feeling at a funeral. I arrived home shortly afterward and told my mother how sick I had felt at work and that I needed a chest X-ray.

My mother was astonished at my need to rush to the hospital because just two weeks before, I had been examined for whooping cough. At that time I had a nonstop cough that I thought I had caught from one of the children at the center. When I told the doctor that I might have caught the cough at the center, he assumed—without doing a thorough diagnosis or X-ray—that I had bronchitis because of my asthma history. He discharged me with a prescription for antibiotics, which did absolutely nothing for me.

My mother and I really hoped to get to the bottom of the situation this time and avoid an unnecessary visit like the last one. When we arrived at the hospital, I had a sudden need to go to the restroom. As I walked into the rest-room, I noticed a lady hunched over the sink, barfing up what seemed to be her entire insides. There was a lot of puke, and her facial expression was full of pain. I asked her if she was okay and if she wanted me to get help, but she told me she was going to be alright. When I met my mother back in the lobby, I described what I had just witnessed. My mother immediately rushed to tell a nurse about the ill woman. The nurse along with a few staff members ran into the bathroom. To my astonishment they came out of the bathroom dumbfounded and confused because there were no signs of puke on the floor or the sink, and the bathroom was empty. I later came to realize the woman was a vision of me being sick and puking from extensive chemotherapy and radiation. I had seen a miraculous vision, and I will never forget the lady who insisted that she would be alright.

When the doctor finally called me into the emergency room, I was shocked by the rude comment he made when I told him about the events at work and how long I had been sick. After hearing about my illness, the doctor asked me if my chest pains could be caused by wearing my bra too tight. Surprised by the comment and not knowing how to react, I overlooked the idiotic question and became serious. I demanded that he order an X-ray.

Three hours went by, and I began to worry because my mother had fallen asleep. I became really nervous and anxious. I knew the news would be bad when the doctor returned because he was taking so long. I put my ear to the hallway and overheard the doctors and nurses say, "The young girl in room five was walking." That was me, and I was nineteen years old at the time. When the doctor came back, the first thing that he said was that he was sorry I was going to have to go through so much to get better. I quickly asked if I could see the X-ray. It looked as if my entire chest cavity was compacted by the tips of branches in winter time when they have no leaves. I'm not and never was a doctor, but I knew a chest was not supposed to look like that. From that point on, my life changed. I received four blood transfusions that night and a lot of tests were done on me. As I recall, I was in this particular hospital for ten days before being transferred to a hospital that specialized in various types of cancer.

In the following weeks I learned that if I did not start chemotherapy soon, I would have, at the most, six weeks to live because Hodgkin's disease was spreading throughout my body, even down to the bone marrow. My spleen was so swollen with the cancerous, compacted tumors in my lymph nodes that the doctors were amazed it had not exploded. What amazed me was that I was born in August and would die in August if I did not get help. My official diagnosis was made on June 24, 2004. I had Stanford 5 chemotherapy, which was an ordeal every Friday for twelve weeks. I started radiation in December 2004. I received it everyday for a month, and was in remission for three months. The cancer came back on my spinal cord. It looked like an infection, but because I did not have a fever, they did another biopsy. The doctors knew it was more than likely to be cancer, which was disturbing because the disease was supposed to be easy to treat. They believed the remission period was short because they had not caught the disease until its final stage. Even after all the chemo and radiation, the cancer still came back because it had adapted to my immune system. I received chemotherapy in September 2005 for six weeks, and then the Hodgkin's disease came back. I am currently receiving a stem-cell transplant and I should officially be finished with this treatment in March 2006. Hopefully I can get some financial assistance with school fees this year. I plan to pick up where I left off in pursuing my goal to finish college with a bachelor's degree.

I am still in a lot of pain from the damage done to my veins at the hospital. They became so battered that nurses couldn't even draw blood with butterfly needles, which they use on infants. I have a med port in my left breast. Two large tubes go through my superior vena cava, and another major artery. All three tubes now rest on the top of my heart, and I have a hard time sleeping because I only sleep comfortably on my stomach.

Throughout this whole process I am very thankful for the faith that I have in Jesus. If it had not been for him, I would not have dreamed about drinking plenty of water, and my spleen would have violently ruptured as the doctor had said. I now make sure that I faithfully go to church to remind myself every week of the power of prayer, of how powerful and almighty God is, and of his never-ending mercy and love.

CHAPTER 2

Visions of a Life

When Shanile was about four years old, she resided in Dover, Delaware with her family. One night she awoke at two o'clock in the morning, and saw a vision of a devilish, green fiend with an evil grin. She started screaming and ran into her mother's room full of fear. Her mother prayed a prayer for Jesus' divine protection to overshadow her daughter, and by the power of God the fiend never came back.

Shanile also shared the Bible with people she did not know, or people she knew who wanted to learn about the Lord. She felt some people treated her as if she were contagious, or as if she had eaten something to get this disease. She did not care how people looked at her. She would never hesitate to share the good news of Christ. She would go out and party with friends and at any moment start preaching about the importance of the Ten Commandments. She would also describe Jesus and his works, being born to a virgin, and the suffering he endured under Pontius Pilate, dying on a cross, crucified, battered torn body full of pain, to give up his life, to save everyone from hell, and his resurrection on the third day to sit at the right hand of the Father. She would tell people to believe this truth and they would be saved by Jesus' blood.

One day Shanile had a vision of a lady talking to her. Her mom and brothers were all at the table praying for her survival. At that very moment Shanile said their voices began to fade and she heard a lady's voice, soft and comforting. The voice told her she was special, the Virgin Mary would be with her mother, her brother Eric would be a comforter, and her brother Michael shared the name of the archangel Michael for a purpose. Shanile and her family believed that this voice was in preparation for the transition to the next life.

CHAPTER 3

Dreaming on a Sick Bed

Shanile woke up one morning and went to her mother and said, "Last night, I had a dream that my spirit came out of my body and was floating in the air." In her dream she looked up and saw a very bright light. She looked down and saw hell. People were trying to climb out and devils would pull them back into the fire-storm in the pit. She focused on the light and went right into it.

As her mother listened to the story, she knew her daughter's time on earth was almost up. God blessed Shanile to let the unbelievers know there is a hell, and Jesus is so kind, holy, and righteous that he does not want anyone to go there. His glorious news brings salvation to all, and will restore the hearts of all unbelievers. God's deliverance, love and forgiveness is represented through his son Jesus Christ, intended for all who embrace this beautiful news that will over shroud our hearts to sheer elation and joy. Christ's love aspire all people to repent of their sins by changing their old ways, and becoming anew in Christ through baptism, and by the receiving of the Holy Spirit.

Shanile also dreamed of becoming a senator. She wanted to graduate from college, keep a full-time job, and serve in the senate. She would work to have laws passed for the elderly, to help them enjoy a better quality of life. Shanile envisioned of working hard to provide children the best resources, as well as opportunities to intellectually grow and excel with their future endeavors. She passionately believed in teaching our youth how important it is to maintain a clean environment. Shanile would ensure the safety of everyone as well as respect for all people. She wanted hospital patients to have the best healthcare and clean rooms. Shanile believed hospital staff should be more understanding about cancer. She believed strongly that hospital staff should not just work for a paycheck, they should offer hope, not make rude remarks. She believed that staff who did not do their jobs would be judged by God when their time comes and they leave this earth. He would judge them right. She said, "Patient abuse must stop! The sick have rights; they are human beings just like you and me."

CHAPTER 4

The Reality of Cancer

Cancer is dark with no light. It comes to steal life that God has made real. It is the thief of the hopes of tomorrow and the next day because it brings sorrow and pain. It will not prevail, though, because the one thing it cannot lay claim to is your soul. God is always the victor! The body is nothing but the dust of the earth. The soul is holy and eternal and bears the love of God.

Cancer forced Shanile's body to undergo horrifying torture. Her skin fell off, and the itch was unbearable. Shanile described it as butterflies fluttering underneath her skin. She lost all of her hair, even her eye lashes. With the slightest brush, locks of hair would fall out. Her skin became as flaky as a barren desert. The pain, the ulcers, and the mistreatment at the hospital all weighed heavily on her shoulders. She still prayed and trusted God with all of her heart. The love she had for God was so great no demon in hell or on earth could touch her faith in God and her courage.

CHAPTER 5

Shanile's Family

Shanile has three brothers: Michael, Eric, and Elijah. Michael is the oldest and two years older than Shanile. He is a graduate of Bowling Green State University with a bachelor's degree in computer science engineering and a minor in business and finance. When they were young, Shanile and Michael were each other's only friend. They were children of the military which meant they would travel frequently. This made them very close. As they settled, Michael began making friends and filling the role of the typical big brother, playing pranks and running around with the boys of the neighborhood. Shanile played the role of the typical little sister, wanting to hang around the big brother. At times their differences would provoke arguments. Michael was very protective of his sister. He liked to have adventures that could be dangerous, such as jumping over a fence to taunt a dog, but he would not let his sister join him in these activities.

One day, when he was seven years old, Michael went off with his friends to pick on a neighborhood dog that barked all day. Shanile asked to go with him, but Michael refused and ran along with his friends. When the boys jumped the fence and opened the gate, they saw to their astonishment that the dog was not chained in its usual location. All of a sudden the dog came racing around the side of the house, unchained and barking. All the boys scattered and Michael ran to jump the fence. The dog was hot in pursuit of Michael when it changed direction. As Michael leapt onto the fence, he turned around to see his sister at the open gate, screaming as the dog leaped on her. Michael jumped down and ran toward the dog. He kicked it, yanked Shanile away and closed the gate. It was at that very moment that Shanile developed a phobia of dogs that would last well into her adult life.

When Michael and Shanile spent time together, a strange connection would always take place. For example, one day when Michael was riding his skateboard, he fell and scraped his knee badly. The next day, Shanile rode her tricycle, fell and bruised herself in exactly the same place as Michael. Every injury or illness suffered by the one was bound to be shared by the other. They often joked about it, calling themselves twins. This connection was also telepathic.

When they were in their teens, Michael and Shanile visited the Wyandot Lake water park. Michael was an okay swimmer, but Shanile could not swim at all. After going on most of the rides, the two decided to go to the wave pool. The wave pool is a large pool that resembles a beach. The pool has a generator to simulate ocean waves. Knowing that the pool is quite deep at the end, the two picked up a two-person, floating tube. The wave pool was very crowded that day and the temperature was approaching eighty degrees. As the generator kicked in, the waves begin to form. The current quickly carried Michael and Shanile out to the deepest area. Michael and Shanile were having a good time, relaxing in the blazing sun. There were so many people in the pool that they could only hear the voice of the person directly next to them. The two began to worry because they were in very deep water, and it was too crowded to try and paddle back to the edge of the pool. As Michael looked around to try and figure out how to get back, he had a very eerie feeling in the pit of his stomach. He turned around to look for Shanile, but she was gone. As he began to panic, he saw a dark image slowly sinking in the water. He let go of the tube and swam down to grab the nearest part of it. It turned out to be a hand. Shanile's hand! As he pulled her onto the tube, she coughed up water and started crying. At that moment a man swam up to the tube and said that it was his. The number on the side indicated so. Michael told the man that he could have it back if he took him and Shanile back to the edge of the pool. The man obliged.

Another telepathic mystery occurred one night in the fall. Michael suddenly awoke at 4 a.m. in a cold sweat. He had the same eerie feeling that he had felt that day in the wave pool. He jumped out of bed and began looking for his shoes and phone. His girlfriend woke up. She was frightened and asked him what was wrong. He told her that something was wrong with his sister. He called Shanile, Eric, and his mom, but no one answered. He called Shanile again and she picked up the phone, frightened. She said that she could not breathe. Michael rushed over to her house. She was calm when he arrived and just smiled when he told her what happened. She said, "I told you we were twins."

Soon after Shanile came down with cancer, it was evident that she would need a stem-cell transplant to survive. The first transplant used her cells and failed. The second transplant had to come from a donor. The doctors said that the highest chance of success would be from a sibling donor's cells, which would limit the risk of rejection. As soon as we heard this news, Shanile and Michael knew that Michael would be the donor. We joked. Twins right? The doctor said that she wanted to test both Michael and Eric. Shanile lost her patience and protested. She did not want Eric tested. She felt it was a waste of time because she knew that Michael was a match. Shanile believed that Michael was blessed by God to be one of her protectors. Eric was also blessed. Shanile and Michael were two years apart in age. Michael who seldom got sick would be her match and his cells would end the cancer. Shanile tried to explain this to the doctor who immediately lost her patience and said that even if Michael's cells matched, the process would still be difficult because Michael and Shanile were not twins. In fact, there was no guarantee that either Michael's or Eric's cells would match, which would mean that Shanile would have to have cells from an unrelated donor. Shanile gave the doctor the "whatever" look and said, "Go ahead and waste your time." The results showed that Eric's cells did not match Shanile's cells, but Michael's matched. The match was so close the doctor admitted it was as if Michael were her twin. The doctor went over the details with Michael. She said the pain would be excruciating and asked if he were sure if he wanted to do it. Michael looked at the doctor and said, "The pain is irrelevant. If this will save my sister's life, please do continue the process and do not ask me this question again. As her brother, I do not have a choice."

The night before the transplant Michael prayed for the procedure to work and fasted. He called his friends over to have a strenuous boxing session. He was very stressed over the transplant process. He knew that he had a very aggressive immune system that matched his personality. He was afraid that his cells might attack Shanile's body or would not be enough to cure the cancer. He felt that if he could get to the point where he didn't want to do anything but give up and in spite of that still continue, he would be able to overcome any hardship. While fasting, he entered a sparring session with his friends Elvin and Quintin. It was 9 p.m. They were told to switch places with each other when one of them grew tired of sparring with Michael, but Michael would not switch with any one. They sparred continuously for two hours as Michael sweated, bled, and wept. When they told Michael to quit, he yelled for them to continue. When he was beyond exhaustion, he wanted the feeling to be remembered by every cell of his body so when his cells entered Shanile, they would fight the cancer until there was no more of it to destroy.

Eric is Shanile's middle brother. He is four years younger than his sister. He was also very protective of her. He always would make sure her friends believed in Jesus— absolutely no boyfriends, only friends. Eric loved his sister very much and is determined to graduate from college in memory of her. He saw Shanile as a soldier of Christ with a stout heart for God, a testimony of faith for all people living in doubt. He believes God Almighty should be praised for everything he has done and will do, for troubles don't last forever.

I am the middle brother, Eric. My sister was determined to win through her battles in life and be free from ungodliness. She once told me that there is only good and evil in this world and nothing between them. You are either with God or you're not. Shanile knew this, and it's even mentioned in the Bible in Matthew 6:24 "No one can serve two masters. For you will hate one and love the other, or be devoted to one and despise the other. You cannot serve both God and money." Shanile stood firm in God's army, carefully awaiting commands from almighty King Jesus to help save the spiritually captive. Shanile became wise each and every day. One of her favorite chapters is from the book of Proverbs 3:1–35. My sister and brothers grew up faithfully believing in God, and through her trials, Shanile proved herself faithful by maintaining her love in Jesus, the lord of lords. Jesus revealed to all of us that he is to be believed because he revealed Shanile to some of her friends and family through dreams and visions. "There is a true saying in Timothy 2:11: "If we die with him, we will also live with him. If we endure hardship, we will reign with him. If we deny him, he will deny us. If we are unfaithful, he remains faithful; for he cannot deny himself."

My big sister began down the road which all Christians have taken: the narrow path, full of light and God's love that begins through Jesus and ends with him and that cannot be walked without him. We need Jesus throughout our times of struggle to endure the challenges of this world. Though it may seem hard and painful, God will always help us in our times of need. We must seek him diligently and make his kingdom our main concern. Christ showed us that even though a Christian may be in a tunnel, Christ will protect him on the way in and out. Christ is the everlasting light when you cannot see, and he will be the light that extinguishes darkness, which may come in the form of bills, disease, school, or even a bully. My sister was true to Jesus and to her family and friends. My sister was full of grace and God-given valor. She was able to endure the pain of cancer, illuminating her life with the unbounded, tender mercies of joy and freedom that are reserved for those who endure times of trial and who, despite the hardship and pain, receive salvation and the crown of life promised to God's people. As a Christian I believe that we must not let disease, financial problems, or peer issues consume us, but rather, we must strengthen ourselves with God's word(truth) and glorify him at all times for the victory he has already been won. Instead of walking with your head low, do the opposite: keep your head up as the Lord guides you. We must all strive to pick up our cross and follow Jesus, the only Son of God and commander of all the armies of heaven.

Lastly, to all Christians going through life's struggles, I say hold on to God's holy anchor of love, which is Christ Jesus, God's greatest gift from above. All those who are struggling to overcome sin and be saved but are afraid to tell anyone or do anything, should think of it this way: When you expose yourself to the light, your spirit is illuminated! To quote John 3:18–21: "There is no judgment awaiting those who trust him. But those who do not trust him have already been judged for not believing in the only Son of God. Their judgment is based on this fact: The light from heaven came into the world, but they loved the darkness more than the light, for their actions were evil. They hate the light because they want to sin in the darkness. They stay away from the light for fear their sins will be exposed and they will be punished. But those who do what is right come to the light gladly, so everyone can see that they are doing what God wants." Again, when you expose yourself to the light, your spirit is no longer in the dark!

This is a poem I wrote to my dear aunt for all of her love and support.

To our Aunt so Gracious with love,
How Sweet she is, God's gift from above,

So wise and blessed to place her fortunes aside
To help her niece with God's love planted inside.
Her heart proves golden; it's an evident fact.
For it was tested, and everything left intact

My sister held on the holy anchor of love,
Which is CHRIST JESUS, God's greatest gift from above,

JESUS allowed her to be an example of God's glorious light
That overshadows everything, even the darkest night,

We thank God for you and for heeding his call,
JESUS' love shines through you and his love completes us all.

In Jesus' name, holy, wondrous God, generations bow before thee. Your grace and power is limitless. Alleluia! Blessings and glory to him. Joy, valor, faithfulness, and awesomeness emanates from him. Amen.

Elijah is Shanile's youngest brother. He was six years old when she passed. She taught him to be strong, always ask questions, and have faith in God in everything he did. He remembers that one day when she was very sick, she still got out of bed to check on him and make sure he was dry and give him his medicine. He cries at times when he misses his sister, but when the sun is shining, he says Shanile is in heaven looking down and smiling at him.

Shanile's mother and father were divorced, but her mother eventually got remarried to a wonderful Christian man, named Kevin. He loved Shanile as if she were his own. When Shanile vomited from the chemo, he would be right there, cleaning up the mess. If she had cravings in the middle of the night, he would go to the store and seek out what she desired. He did everything a good father would do for his child.

CHAPTER 6

Peace Granted to a Sorrowful Mother

One night, I was so sad. It was the kind of sadness that brings on a headache. I was sad about the loss of my beautiful daughter, Shanile. I fell on my knees and had a talk with God. I said, "Father, in the name of Jesus, let my daughter come back to me. I am sorry for my sins." Well, when I went to bed, I had a dream of peace and love that only Jesus can give. In the dream I saw my daughter walking. She was dressed like a model. Her hair had grown back. I said, "Shanile?" She turned around and ran to me. When we embraced, I felt her face and said, "Shanile, you are alive?" She said, "Mommie, look at me. Jesus has resurrected me, Mommie." Then she turned around and said, "Mommie, I can move now because Jesus lives inside me." I was so shocked at those words that when

I woke up, I fell on my knees and had another talk with God. I said, "Lord, thank you for giving me peace and love. Thank you for having mercy on me and forgiving me, for I will love you forever. My soul is signed, sealed, and delivered to you, Lord Jesus Christ.

chapter 7

A Last Applause for the Church

Good Shepherd Lutheran Church

Thank you so much for everyone's support, concerns, and blessings. All of God's anointed people are definitely part of the Good Shepherd Family.

Reformation Family Church

I love Jesus. I asked him a favor: to keep me with the people I love until I am ready to go with him. He listened to me and has delivered me from all evil.

Shanile Sharay Goggins

CHAPTER 8

Shanile's Favorite Prayer

The Lord is my Shepherd. I shall not want. He maketh me to lie down in green pastures; He leadeth me beside the still waters. He restoreth my soul. He leadeth me by the paths of righteousness for his name sake. Yea, though I walk through the valley of the shadow of death, I will fear no evil. For thou art with me. Thy rod and thy staff shall comfort me. For thou preparest a table before me in the presence of my enemies. Thou annointest my head with oil; my cup runneth over. Surely goodness and mercy shall follow me all the days of my life. And I will dwell in the house of the Lord forever and ever. Amen

This was Shanile's favorite prayer, which she chose to say everyday. It is quoted from Psalm 23.

CHAPTER 9

A Family Says Thank You

We thank God for granting us the blessing of having Shanile in our family and ending her suffering in this life. We would like to thank Cynthia Slate, Shanile's aunt for all of her love and her support. I would like to thank the rest of our family, and also our friends for all of their support and the long hours they spent with Shanile in her last weeks in this life. We are forever grateful.

A special thank you goes out to Shanile's pastor, Kathy, and her friends. Thank you for the support and generosity you showed Shanile as she passed to her eternal home. To have you all in her life is a blessing that only God can give. To the good nurses and doctors, thank you for your hard work.

LaVergne, TN USA
08 July 2010
188870LV00001B/1/P